Real Life
Stories
About Our
Real Life
God

Rhonda,
You are such an
inspiration! I love
your heart!
Love in Christ,
Carly

CARLY VAN LAAR

For my family who has been so patient with me on this journey. For my husband, Brandon, who has encouraged and challenged me throughout this past year. For my son, who is among my biggest supporters. Thank you for getting so excited each time you found me writing. For my daughter, with your sweet hugs, kisses, and affirmation.

For my mom, who was quick to read each blog post and help with grammatical issues, providing support and encouragement along the way.

For Wanda, who is without a doubt my biggest "book cheerleader"! Thank you for your encouragement to get me to this point.

For the one person who deepens their relationship with Christ, or the one who comes to know Jesus as their Lord and Savior. This book is absolutely for you, and you were in my mind through all the long hours spent in front of the computer. If this is you, I would absolutely love to hear from you!

For my Lord. I don't know why you chose to use me, but I am so very grateful. It is my prayer that You alone are glorified through this book. You are my everything.

CONTENTS

INTRODUCTION

I loathe writing. Really. I do. In fact, when I taught 5th grade and had to prepare the students for the standardized writing test, I wanted to pat each of their heads and say, "I'm so sorry I'm making you do this."

This is where God has a sense of humor. Why? Because He has lead me to share Him with others through written words. He knows that I will have to continually depend on Him to do this. He will be made perfect in my weakness.

I began by sharing my heart through personal Facebook posts and through weekly emails to the parents at the preschool where I work. Early on in this journey, there has been NO DOUBT that I was being obedient to God. Over and over, I had this confirmed through different people. People would tell me in person to not stop writing/sharing, that they were proud of me for doing what I was doing. One person told a mutual friend, "Please tell your friend not to stop sharing." Facebook messages were sent with encouragement from people telling me what they are learning about God through my posts.

Okay, God, you are coming in loud and clear!

I received encouragement to broaden my audience. Whew, that's a tough one. It's one thing to share on Facebook with my friends, it's quite another to put myself out there on the World Wide Web. (Just typing those words made me hear the old dial-up tone in my head!)

So, I prayed and sought God's will for this. You guys, boy, did He ever answer! Within a couple days, I had a ministry name & I could "see" the logo that would go with it. "Loved Fiercely Ministries". I thought it was a perfect ministry name, pointing to just how much God loves us. Again, wanting to make sure that this was God, and not me, I stopped to pray about it again. The next morning, a friend had posted the following on Facebook under my post that ended with the tag line featured under the logo on my website:

"Thank you again for your posts. Your sharing of these is a way of witnessing, not only to those who don't know our Savior, but to those of us that need to be reminded of how awesome He is and the work he does in our lives because he loves us 'fiercely'. I needed this."

There it was. Confirmation to go ahead with the name, "Loved Fiercely".

That morning, as I was getting ready for work, I was praying over the "reveal" of my website, and I kept picturing Bambi's mom from the Disney movie. Remember when Bambi wanted to explore the meadow, but his mom warned him not to go into the meadow, for he would be exposed, that the meadow is dangerous? That was the image on repeat in my head. BUT, the "funny" thing is that every time I pictured this, right behind it, I pictured my Lord leading me into that meadow. It was His out-stretched hand reaching back for me to follow Him there. I firmly believe that He was preparing me for what might come once I put myself "out there". With this image, I have no fear, and I know I'm supposed to follow Him into the "meadow" of the World Wide Web.

Okay, get ready...you won't believe this....mid-morning on that same day, I receive this text from a friend:

"Hey, sisterfriend! Just want to let you know that God kept showing me your sweet smiling face this morning so I am making it my given job from Him to pray for you today and praise Him for you. He told me to specifically pray for protection for you from spiritual warfare. That as you are walking in such faith to share your heart for Him and broaden your "Publix Ministry" Satan wants to make you stumble and fail. Please know you can keep walking straight today, eyes focused on His glory and no need to look down for stumbling stones, or to look right or left for oncoming distractions. If there is anything else I can be lifting up today, just let me know and it will be an honor to do so. Be blessed, dear Carly!!!"

You guys, she had NO IDEA that I was

planning on broadening my "ministry". I truly wanted to fall down and worship my Lord right there for having her pray for me. How indescribably amazing is our God!!! After telling her what I just shared with you, she had more encouragement and then ended with this:

"Now, get your fanny out there in that meadow and freely run through the grass with full abandon towards Him – ya know, like little Laura Ingalls running down that hill at the start of "Little House on the Prairie"."

Okay, so there I was about to make the website public, running with full abandon into the meadow. Following my Lord.

He wants you to follow Him too. With every step you take. Come to the meadow with me. You won't regret it

"I will lift up my eyes to the mountains;
From where shall my help come? My help *comes* from the Lord,
Who made heaven and earth.
He will not allow your foot to slip;
He who keeps you will not slumber.
Behold, He who keeps Israel
Will neither slumber nor sleep.

The Lord is your keeper;
The Lord is your shade on your right hand.
The sun will not smite you by day,
Nor the moon by night.

The Lord will protect you from all evil;
He will keep your soul.
The Lord will guard your going out and your coming in
From this time forth and forever."
Psalm 121

The blog website opened more doors, which has been amazing. I share only what God has laid on my heart. The website was launched in November 2015, and by end of summer 2016, there were stirrings in my heart about putting the blog posts in book format. Once I finally submitted to the stirrings, there was a peace. Knowing I was in the will of God, has made the extra time to publish manageable. As you recently read on the dedication page, this book is for the one person who may come to know Jesus as their Savior, for that one person is absolutely loved and created by a God who desires that he/she come to know Him as their Savior.

Soooooooo, here we are!

Thank you for purchasing this book, for reading it, for gifting it to others. Trust me when I say that your support is amazing! Thank you!

www.lovedfiercely.wordpress.com

My Temper-Tantrum with God

This is a long, personal one. God really laid it on my heart to "get real" and share a skeleton from my closet, so get comfy, settle in and allow me tell you about the time that I turned my back on God.

Have you ever encountered a spoiled child? Have you ever been around when that child was told "no"? What happened? I can only imagine that it would be a temper-tantrum, right?

Well, I learned that I was a spoiled child. A spoiled-child-of-God, that is.

Let's begin at the beginning.... I grew up in a home where both my parents were Christian. We went to church every time the doors were opened. I learned early on that the Bible said that "All have sinned and fall short of the glory of God" (Rom. 3:23). I knew at the age of five that I sinned, and therefore I needed a Savior. My mom used to tell me that even as a 5-year-old at Christmastime, I would pray to "my Lord" & not "Baby Jesus". I made my decision to follow Jesus public at the age of 6 (I walked the aisle of my church at invitation time and told my pastor, who shared it with the people gathered in church that day), and I was baptized at the age of seven. In our faith, baptism is not required for salvation, but it is a public way of acknowledging that I was born again, that is, born into the kingdom of God, demonstrating that my old life was buried (going under the water) and my new life has begun (coming up out of the water).

I was surrounded by lots of people who helped in grow in my walk with Christ. I still remember precious Sunday School teachers who helped me learn God's word and made me hungry for God's word. One person, however, impacted my walk with Christ tremendously...my dad.

My dad demonstrated what it meant to love as Christ loves. My dad poured everything he had into serving Christ. I remember seeing him in times of prayer laying face down, pouring his heart out. I remember seeing him with a small reading light on at night reading his bible in bed. My dad taught an adult Sunday School class, was a deacon in our church, and cried every time the Spirit moved him. Wanting to share the gospel further, my dad organized an outdoor Passion Play involving seven area churches & it took place in my hometown of downtown Norcross. My dad was a full-time Kroger Pharmacist, then later was also a seminary student, and part-time associate pastor. Jesus was his passion. Jesus was always on his lips. Then, when him and my mom were in the hills of Kentucky scouting out a mission trip opportunity, my dad suffered a massive stroke. With no hospital close. This stroke robbed my of my dad. It took his voice. It took his right side movement. This was the year 2000, he was 48 years old. My dad is still with us, but unfortunately, I can no longer have those awesome, in-depth bible discussions with him. This all fits into my story---I promise.

Back to my spoiled-child-of-God state... My only job interview was at the age of fifteen at Chick-fil-A. I was recruited from there to Atlanta Sports & Rec. My now husband, Brandon, was also recruited there, and this is where we met (when I was 16 & he was 20). Because I sought the will of God at EVERY turn, I knew that I was supposed to attend the University of Georgia upon graduation. So, I only filled out one college application, and was accepted. (My parents were Auburn grads, but my dad said he would learn to bark like a dawg for the HOPE scholarship.) Brandon transferred to UGA from the community college in town, and we both came to Athens in 1997. Without a doubt, I knew I heard the voice of God in my freshman English class in Park Hall telling me that Brandon was the one I was supposed to marry.

We were engaged at the end of my freshman year and we were married when I was 20, in May of 1999.

My degree was in education, and I student taught at County Line Elementary, where I was then hired as a 5th grade teacher.

Brandon and I joined Green Acres Baptist Church and were in the newlywed class.

Life was good. Life was great! God had directed my path at every. single. turn. I trusted Him with everything. My favorite verse is: "Trust in the Lord with all your heart and lean not on your own understanding. In all your ways acknowledge Him and He will direct your path." Proverbs 3:5-6.

I found this verse to be tried and true.

Then, after four years of marriage, we were ready to start our family.

And God said no.

I didn't understand what was happening. What was God doing? We were ready to become become pregnant and it wasn't happening. So I prayed. And prayed harder. And nothing. So, I did what any spoiled child would do. I threw a temper-tantrum. And turned my back on God.

In our newlywed class, other couples around us were getting pregnant. It was too hard for me to be around them, so we quit attending church. I quit reading my bible. I quit praying. For a child who literally grew up knowing and loving God, this was new territory for me.

Time had passed, so my doctors were now ready to explore and do some testing. My tests turned out fine. Brandon's test turned out fine. There was something small that it could be, but all in all, everything looked good. Instead of rejoicing in this fact, my heart grew harder toward God. "See, God, I KNEW this was You."

Advice was given to "quit trying so hard". Take your mind off it. Fully submit to God. I tried all these things, but I was only faking it. I couldn't take my mind off of something that I wanted so badly. I had previously poured out the entire contents of my heart to God and He didn't care, so that didn't work either.

Again time passed and a procedure was scheduled--an insemination (turkey baster kind of thing). I was given one round of Clomid (a fertility drug), to ensure that I had eggs for the procedure. I now knew the date that I was going to become pregnant!!! I couldn't wait!!! I scheduled a sub for my classroom and took the whole day off!

In the doctor's office, everything was set. I was set up for an ultrasound, which showed five eggs! The technician began to take measurements on each egg to make sure they were ready for the procedure. However, none of them were ready. They needed 24 more hours to mature, and this was a Friday, so the office was closed the next day, being Saturday.

My hopes deflated. As we walked out of the office, everything was a blur. Brandon tried to comfort me, but I seriously was like a zombie. I was numb. How could this be?!? This was the date that I had looked forward to for so long. I was completely broken.

Brandon went back to work, and since I had taken the entire day off, I went home. Still numb, I let our dog, Bailey, out into the backyard to do her business. At this time, we lived in a neighborhood in Statham, and our unfenced wooded backyard backed up to a cow pasture. Bailey would always dash out of the house, into the woods to go tell those cows who was boss. She did this every single time, which created a well-worn path into the woods.

I followed her and being completely overwhelmed by the news I had just encountered, I fell apart. I whispered to God, "I need you."

Instantly, I felt the overwhelming presence of my Lord and Savior. There are truly no words to describe what I felt, but it is just like the old hymn says, "He walks with me, and talks with me, and tells me I am one of His own." I sobbed and sobbed and was comforted. I didn't know how, but I knew I was going to be okay. Even if I never became pregnant, Jesus was enough. He alone completely filled me up. I didn't want to leave the woods that afternoon. I poured my heart out to God. I apologized for turning my back. I couldn't believe that after all that time away from Him, that all I had to do was whisper to Him and He was there.

When Brandon came home, I was a completely different person than the one he had left in the parking lot of the doctor's office. I was truly changed. I was ready to trust God's plan for my life again, even if that plan meant no children of our own.

Really long story short; we got pregnant that weekend. On our own, not in a doctor's office. When we went back for our first doctor appointment to confirm the pregnancy, we saw not one, but two babies. We had one boy and one girl. When we found out their genders, I sobbed and sobbed once again. This time it was tears of humbleness. My faithful God, whom I had turned my back on, chose to bless us with one of each. I felt so very undeserving. Not a day goes by that I do not thank God for my children.

I also thank God for that season of trying. I never in-a-million-years thought I would be thankful for that season, but it was that season that taught me the most about God. It taught me how to trust, even when I cannot see. It taught me about God's sovereignty. This spoiled-child-of-God is now grateful that God said no. For it was in that "no", that I grew the most.

It's in that "no" that makes me continue to pray for my dad, even after 16+ years. I may never get to hear my dad preach again this side of heaven. But what do I know? I know that God loves me like no other. He has a reason for not choosing to heal my dad. And I will trust that reason, even though I don't know what it is. I also know that my dad will spend eternity in heaven where he will have a brand new body. Where he will be able to lift both hands and his voice in praise to God. This life is short. Heaven is eternal. God is awesome.

"For I know that ALL things work together for good, for those who are called according to His purpose." Romans 8:28

Are you called for His purpose? Are you known by Him? If not, don't delay another moment, surrender to Christ. I 100% guarantee that you will not regret it and that your life will be changed in amazing ways.

Publix Ministry Story

I've always had the desire to share the Good News of Jesus with people I encounter, I just didn't know how to do it. I've read books (a favorite is <u>Out of the Saltshaker & into the World</u>), and I've searched stories of people who witness to others, but nothing helped with the conversations I was having. You see, I was missing THE most important component, the Holy Spirit.

In the past, I was literally forcing the conversation when it really didn't fit. It was awkward and uncomfortable--for us both.

So recently, I've prayed for boldness to share Christ and to be sensitive to when His Spirit prompts. I wait upon the Lord before moving forward with a conversation about Him. I'd love to share with you how it is very different when I am obedient to do this....

On this particular day, I had prayed for boldness and sensitivity to the Spirit while I was getting ready for my day. The day had really passed like any other day, until I was at Publix and unloading my cart onto the conveyor belt. This was when I felt the unmistakable nudge from above.

Now, let's talk about what that means with me. You know when you are on a roller coaster, and your gut feels like it has sank to your feet? Yep, that. That's what I do when I feel the Spirit nudging me. It's different for everyone, and boy, I wish it was different for me. I hate roller coasters and I like my gut to stay right where it is, thank you very much.

No!, I thought. Not now. It's crowded tonight, and I've got way too many coupons! (Being behind a couponer in line is not a pleasant place to be for some people.) But, okay, I will be obedient. So, I consented to the Spirit and voiced a silent prayer letting God know that I was willing to go wherever He led the conversation.

As I stood at the checkout station, I wondered how in the world this door of conversation was going to open, when the cashier, a young guy in his early 20's, (we'll call him "Young Publix Guy" or YPG for short) replied back a greeting when a gentlemen walking by said "hello" to him.

I said, "How nice that customers are so friendly here."

He said, "Well, he goes to my church."

Me: "What church do you go to?"

He told me that he attended a local baptist church.

Me: "Oh thank goodness! I was feeling totally prompted by the Holy Spirit to share my faith, but you've already heard the gospel! Now, I don't have to."

Being real with you all, relief poured over me, and I asked him, "Why is it that we are so timid to share the Good News of Christ with others?"

YPG looked at me like I had grown two heads, as did the others in line around me, and I don't think he knew just how to respond to me (familiar territory with me), so I continued, "You know, if there was a meteorite headed this way and all these folks were in danger, we'd be sharing like wildfire to warn people, but we don't do that with the Gospel."

YPG says, "That's so true. Something to think about."

At this point, the bagger, a seasoned gentleman (We'll call him Seasoned Publix Guy, SPG for short), asked me, "Have you been able to totally submit to God and His plans for you?"

Me after reflecting for a moment: "Actually, I have, but it wasn't an easy prayer to say. I have children, and saying that prayer meant that if God called me somewhere away from them, I would have to go, but yes, I've done it, have you?"

SPG: "Oh, no ma'am. I can't do that yet. But, I'm learning more about Him everyday."

Me: "That's a wonderful place to start."

And since the transaction was finished, we said our goodbyes and goodnights and the "come again soons" and it ended there. It wasn't awkward. It wasn't forced. It was actually pleasant. Even with the wide eyes I received. This was because it was the Holy

Spirit and not me. Learning from this, I've let the Spirit take the driver's seat and allow Him to lead me, so I can follow where He's already been working & preparing the way.

The next week during my shopping trip, I caught eyes with YPG from a few check-out lines away. He waved and smiled. He remembered. And maybe, just maybe, he's been bold enough to share with others that have come through his line.

I don't know exactly what the Spirit was doing through the conversation, but that's not for me to know. All I have to know is that I need to be sensitive and obedient when the Spirit prompts.

I know that there have been so many times that I have failed at this, and that's why I'm so very glad that God's mercies are new each morning.

"But you will receive power when the Holy Spirit has come upon you; and you shall be My witnesses both in Jerusalem, and in all Judea and Samaria, and even to the remotest part of the earth." Acts 1:8

Have you received the power of the Holy Spirit by submitting your life to Christ? If so, ask to be lead. Tap into that power. You just might be the one to carry a message to someone that will change their life for all eternity. How awesome is that?!

God, You Want Me to Give Away Bacon?

You will not even believe this particular day I had! Believe me, I wouldn't have believed my day if I didn't experience it for myself.

This morning, I had some extra time before leaving (which is shocking news), so I decided to make a bacon, egg and cheese sandwich. Now, before you get too impressed, I had fried the bacon over the weekend. Out of habit, I always cut my sandwiches in half before enjoying them. After polishing off the first half, God told me to give the other half away.

But, God, this is real bacon. Like. Real. Bacon. (I wanted to make sure He knew just what He was asking of me, which He obviously did, cuz He is God.) I decided that I would ask the person if she even *liked* bacon, and if she didn't, that would mean it would be okay to finish it off myself. So, I carefully wrapped the sandwich in a paper towel and headed out the door.

A couple of times a week, I have the pleasure of having a cutie pie ride with me to the preschool where I work. This cutie pie's mom is Wonder Woman. If you think I'm kidding, I'm not. This mom has six kids, and four of them are six-month-old quadruplets. She is AMAZING! So amazing that she was coming through the car rider line at our half day preschool with four adorable babies in four infant carriers! Can you just take a moment to appreciate how much time that takes? I'll wait. Soak that in. Okay, now that you're there, you can see why I wanted to lighten her load by making a schedule to help out with rides to/from preschool.

This was who God wanted me to share my sandwich with. So, when I pulled into her driveway and she's there with cutie pie and his carseat (and she's SHOWERED...I told you...Wonder Woman!), I ask her,
"Do you like bacon, egg, cheese sandwiches?".

She replied, "Who doesn't?!".....my kind of girl! God nailed it and I was so happy I could share with her!

At preschool, I told my friend, "Someone is bringing me breakfast today."

She asks, "Who?"

I reply, "I don't know."

After giving me a questioning look (remember, I'm quite used to these by now-- Jesus followers look really weird sometimes), she asked, "Then, how do you know someone is bringing it?"

"Because God told me to give half of my breakfast away, so I know that He's going to provide somehow."

Let me just tell you that God took my half of a sandwich and turned it into a homemade sour cream biscuit and a Chick-fil-A iced coffee WITH whipped cream! How awesome is God?! Seriously?! NEVER cease to be amazed by Him.

See? I told you my day would be hard to believe! I was faithful with half of a sandwich and God provided.

"He who is faithful in a very little thing is faithful also in much; and he who is unrighteous in a very little thing is unrighteous also in much."   Luke 16:10

Be faithful. You won't regret it.

Fingerprints of God

My dad had a wild ride in an ambulance in the Fall of 2015 when he was unresponsive.

(Quick recap that you'll need to know: my dad suffered a massive stroke at the age of 48 in the year 2000. Physical therapy worked wonders for his body the first eight years, but to maintain a pain-free quality of life, narcotics have been used to manage his pain for the past seven years.)

My dad's restoration from his stroke is a long-term prayer request of mine. Lately, I've been waking up with the hope of: "Lord! This could be the day that you restore my dad!" Now, I did not get to this way of hope overnight. It came through a big learning lesson on trusting the sovereignty of God. (This story is found on pg.7.)

On this particular day, I woke up with this same expectancy. I was unable to go to work, because my daughter had run a mild fever the evening before. We were able to spend a low-key day together and take an unheard-of-afternoon-nap (fingerprint: God knew I would need this rest). On Wednesday nights, I lead the "Sparkies" group at church (K-2nd graders), but since I had a recovering child at home, my husband, Brandon, was filling in for me (fingerprint: God knew I'd be less likely to leave a commitment, especially if I was already there).

I had been talking to my mom earlier in the afternoon, and she was telling me that dad was much less active/awake, which is not terribly uncommon. Anyone who cares for someone long-term (especially with a brain injury) knows that there are good days and bad days. Later, however, she had called me back and said that she was really worried because she couldn't rouse dad and was going to call 911, at which point, I called my sister to let her know. A short time later, I received another phone call, this time from my mom who was fighting back tears, from inside the ambulance where I could hear the sirens wailing, and the loud horn as they were flying through intersections.

You see, the paramedics couldn't rouse my dad either.

I told my mom, "It's going to be okay. No matter what, all will be okay." I had put on my "big girl" gear and steadied myself to be strong for my mom. When I called my sister, however, that strong fortitude fell, and I broke down as I told her what was happening. I did, however, tell her the same reassurance I had told my mom.

How did I *know* that it was going to be okay? Because, you see, whichever way this hospital trip ended, in either scenario, my dad would be restored. He would either be restored here on earth by becoming conscious again, or he would have the ULTIMATE restoration with his new body in heaven. I was absolutely prepared for either of these, whichever scenario God picked, for I trust Him completely.

I called Brandon to let him know that I needed to head to the hospital, and amazing people at our church completely dropped all to fill in for him, who was filling in for me at home. It was already a low-volunteer night at church for illness, and prior commitments, but awesomely, the night had gone so smooth (yet another fingerprint of God), so much so, that our children's minister was able to testify how awesome our God is!

The hospital was an hour away, but I was making great time. It was forecasted for thunderstorms, but not a drop fell from the sky (another fingerprint) and the sky was actually a beautiful canvas of God's handiwork. This made it very easy to pray my whole way in. I broke down once, recalling the last phone conversation with my dad. He had called me during the bonfire we had with our church, and I told him that I couldn't talk, but that I would call him back on my way home, which I forgot to do. Not too long after those thoughts crossed my mind, my mom let me know that dad was conscious, and that they were sending him for a CT scan to see if the lack of oxygen had damaged any more of his brain.

I called my sister, Ashley, (who was an hour away from the opposite direction), and we breathed a collective sigh of relief. When we arrived at the hospital, dad was in a lot of pain, as he had been given a narcotic-blocking drug, which brought consciousness, along with every ounce of pain that the drugs had been blocking. I went straight to his side, purse on my shoulder and all, and My dad, who loves his Lord so, calmed while I prayed over him. I told him that we would have to depend on The Great Physician to take his pain while we waited on the hospital pharmacy to get the order. (Since the stroke affected my dad's right side, he drags his right arm and leg. If you could just let your arm fall limp at your side for a moment, you can image the pain that would cause on your shoulder, and then your hip and knee). There were other happenings that involved all three of us (mom, sis, and I) wearing gloves and making dad more comfortable, but these happenings are best left un-detailed. Trust me.

I know without a doubt that it was the power of prayer that calmed him. I had received a message that the Sparkies prayed for my dad that night. Children praying touches my soul like nothing else, so of course, I had to let a few happy tears fall. The CT and blood work came back fine, and dad was released that same night. Side effects of his pain meds will be watched for closely.

After dad calmed, my sister and I were able to catch up while waiting at the hospital (her living two hours away is two hours too long). She was sharing how she's been struggling with a prayer request, but just felt as if her prayers weren't being heard. She was very real with mom and I, when she told us that she had been tempted to ask God for a sign that He was hearing her. She had also told us about her last 24 hours, and she was able to see where God had directed her path. Come take a peek with me at her events:

-The night before, even though she had 44 miles left on her tank of gas, for some reason she felt the urge to stop and fill up (God know that she'd want to get to the hospital as soon as possible.)

-That day, for some reason, she had put a meal in the crock-pot, even though her husband is the cook in their house; so her and her girls had already eaten dinner when I called her (God knew there would be no time for dinner before Ash had dropped the girls off at a sweet neighbor's house, so she could leave.)

-Earlier in the week, for some reason, they worked on her daughter's homework for the whole week (God knew to take away the homework stress.)

I'd say that God had shown up for Ashley. I'd say that He is listening, but wanting her to wait upon Him.

Can you see these fingerprints? I say all the time that God is always 100 steps ahead of me. Sure, some could say that these are all just coincidence, but not to me. To me, these are God directing our paths.

So, what now? Now, I will continue to wait upon the Lord and wake up again tomorrow with the expectancy that this just might be the day that my prayers are answered. For, I know that in waiting upon the Lord for this prayer request, that He will give me strength. That He will mount me up with wings like eagles. That I will be able to run this life and not grow tired. For my strength comes from Him. What better place for strength to come from?

If you need to be strengthened in this life (who doesn't?!), surrender your life/plans/hopes/dreams to God. Then, look back on events and see His fingerprints. Your maker loves you fiercely. So fiercely, that He gives us the choice to follow Him, or not. Follow Him, trust me, you won't regret it.

"Yet those who wait for the Lord
Will gain new strength,
They will mount up with wings
like eagles,
They will run and not get tired,
They will walk and not become weary."
Isaiah 40:31

Nothing to Give

What if you have nothing to give God? Nothing to present to Him as an offering?

When I was in middle school, my parents had their own business, a Pharmacy/Soda Fountain. The building had been in my family since 1885 as a hardware store. When my grandparents died, my dad, a pharmacist, and my mom, a home-economics major, kept "the store", as we call it, in the family.

But, in the early 1990's, it was hard for a "mom and pop" pharmacy to make it, as all insurance companies do not support non-chain pharmacies. Money became tighter and tighter. Hand-me-down clothes were worn by my sister and I, there were no family vacations, and all non-essential items were cut from the budget.

There was no income coming in. Once savings accounts were also depleted, there was no tithe money. This killed my dad. My parents always taught about how tithing was so important. I saw how God provided for them over and over. But what do you do when you have nothing to give?

You give God your praise. My dad had a song that he LOVED during this short period in our lives. I don't know the title, or the artist, but I know the lines; here's one:
"If it's Praise You Want, Lord I'll praise You."

This song was on repeat. He played it

all. the. time. This man poured out his praise to God when there was nothing else to give. My parents taught my sister and I to praise God, how to pray, how to be thankful.

But what if you can't praise God either? What if you are in a storm of life, and you can't see where you *could* praise God?

Look outside.

As I was getting ready for work on this particular day, the sky was GOURGEOUS! I couldn't help but stop and praise God for his handiwork! He's the ultimate artist! My description could never do it justice, but as the sun was rising, there was a grayish cloud cover that cast such beautiful sun rays across the multi-colored leaves.

Even when "life" tries to get in the way of our praise, by looking outside---at the sky, at the clouds, at the trees, you can find something to praise God for. Try it. You'll be in a different frame of mind when you bring praise to the Lord.

If you don't, the rocks will:

"As soon as He was approaching, near the descent of the Mount of Olives, the whole crowd of the disciples began to praise God joyfully with a loud voice for all the miracles which they had seen, shouting:
"Blessed is the King who comes in the name of the Lord;

Peace in heaven and glory in the
        highest!"
Some of the Pharisees in the crowd said
to Him, "Teacher, rebuke Your
disciples." But Jesus answered, "I tell
you, if these become silent, the stones
will cry out!"
Luke 19:37-39

In case you are curious....what
happened with "the store"?

My dad had previously been a Kroger
Pharmacist before "the store". Just in the
knick of time (which, I've discovered, is
exactly how God likes to operate), a
representative with Kroger came to "the
store". Kroger offered to buy our prescription
drug inventory and offered to reinstate my
dad's years of service. It would be like he
never left Kroger to do "the store".

The big picture view....had dad not
been with Kroger at the time of his stroke, he
would not have had the benefits that working
for a large company offers...no disability
payments, and certainly not the level of
health insurance.

My parents praised God when there
was nothing to give and my, how God
provided.

By the way, the Kroger representative
came to the store on Christmas Eve Day. This
was my most memorable Christmas. One

where we celebrated God's gifts---the gift of His son, Jesus, the gift of providing for our family. We didn't need gifts under the tree.

Be faithful. Give, even when there's nothing to give. Praise God, even through storms. You won't regret it.

> "Enter His gates with thanksgiving And His courts with praise. Give thanks to Him, bless His name. For the LORD is good; His lovingkindness is everlasting And His faithfulness to all generations."
> Psalm 100:4-5

"I'm trying to avoid your wrath."

That's what my son said to me last night. You see, I went on a mom rampage. What's a "mom rampage", you ask? It's where you deal with those things that you say to your children over and over and over.

Last night it was the lack of clearing dishes from the dinner table and the lack of taking items up the stairs that sent me into my mom rampage. That's not too much to ask, right?

Nothing really happened and no child was punished, but my "mom tone" was definitely in use at the lack of obedience. Once the "mom tone" is in use, miraculously, things get picked up so very quickly!

When I made my way upstairs, I found my son on his bed tucked up into his covers. I asked him what he was doing and he answered, "I'm trying to avoid your wrath."

Smart kid.

Lying low was a good choice.

I asked him how many times I've reminded him about clearing dishes and carrying things upstairs. He replied, "about a million". Yep, seems about right to me. We cuddled and said prayers and ended the evening on a good note. I love that kid and no amount of disobedience will ever change my love for him.

Man, that's exactly how God's love

works for us, isn't it? He loves us no matter what. He sent His Son to die for us, even with knowing the sins we would commit.

But, we can't hide from God or His wrath. In my Precious Moments bible from when I was a little girl, is a drawing of a child hiding under the bed covers, and caption says, "YOU CAN'T HIDE FROM GOD"

I think I have every one of those pictures sealed in my head, especially this one. I knew early on that I could hide nothing from God. He sees all, and no amount of avoiding can get me out of that fact. He sees my good. He sees my bad. He sees my ugly. And He loves me still.

Since I am a born-again Christian, He has forgiven my sins. Without this fact, I would not be able to bear the burden of my sins. There are many. Yet, He has forgiven them and separated them as far as the east is from the west.

> "He has removed our sins as far from us as the east is from the west."
> Psalm 103:12

Do you seek to unleash the burden of your sin? Precious one, don't carry it around anymore. Surrender to the Lord. Trust me, you won't regret it. After all, He already knows what we've done. Might as well go ahead and confess. You'll feel so much better and your heavenly Father will rejoice with you over your freedom from your sins.

Lord, forgive me. I make mistakes every single day. Every single hour. Sometimes, in every minute. Lord, I know that Jesus has paid my sin-debt. Thank you for this incredible gift. Thank you that your mercy is new every morning, because you know I need it. Thank you for seeing my all and loving me still. Your love is amazing. The amount of your love is sometimes so very hard to understand. How you can forgive a sinner such as myself is indescribable. Lord, help me to live like you want me to live. Help me to be kingdom-focused. Please, Lord, help me to know your will for the rest of my day today, and then to do it. Make me bold for you. In Jesus name I pray, Amen.

"The LORD'S lovingkindnesses indeed
      never cease,
      For His compassions never fail.
They are new every morning;
      Great is Your faithfulness.
'The LORD is my portion,' says my
      soul,
      'Therefore I have hope in Him.'
The LORD is good to those who wait
      for Him,
      To the person who seeks Him."
Lamentations 3:22-25

Tuck it Away

I encountered my most favorite sentence of the Christmas season on Sunday, when it was read during the lighting of the Advent candle:

"But Mary treasured all these things, pondering them in her heart."

Here's the entire passage:

"When the angels had gone away from them into heaven, the shepherds *began* saying to one another, 'Let us go straight to Bethlehem then, and see this thing that has happened which the Lord has made known to us.' So they came in a hurry and found their way to Mary and Joseph, and the baby as He lay in the manger. When they had seen this, they made known the statement which had been told them about this Child. And all who heard it wondered at the things which were told them by the shepherds. **But Mary treasured all these things, pondering them in her heart.** The shepherds went back, glorifying and praising God for all that they had heard and seen, just as had been told them."

Luke 2:15-20 (emphasis mine)

In all that was happening around Mary at the moment, she paused. She treasured. She pondered. All in her heart.

This is my favorite verse of the season because I love what this amazing mom modeled for me. She had a lot going on around her...she had given birth (in a barn!), some shepherds had just rushed in and were talking, making known what had been told to them, and in all this, she took the time to tuck the moment away. To treasure it and ponder it in her heart.

If Mary could do this under these happenings, could I do it?

I've challenged myself this season to be diligent about treasuring moments and pondering them in my heart to keep my focus on what Mary was treasuring and pondering in her heart.

Last weekend, my family decorated our tree. As I unwrapped my favorite ornament, a church I had painted in middle school, I could see Jesus. God's church (the people, not the building), has meant so much to me throughout my life. Then, when I watched as my children hung ornaments on the tree representing moments in their life, I could see Jesus. Those of you who know our journey to parenthood, know this to be true. I tucked it all away. Treasuring it. Pondering it in my heart.

Our Children's Minister hosted a

Christmas party at her house. There, I paused and pondered about all these amazing harvesters for the Kingdom of God, thanking the Lord for them. As I looked around her home at all the people mingling, eating, servant hearts refilling delicious goodies, I could see Jesus in all of it. I tucked it away. Treasuring it. Pondering it in my heart.

Later that week, we had our Church Weekday Preschool Christmas party at a restaurant. As I sat around the long table with the thirteen other ladies I have the privilege of working with, hearing their laughter, telling memorable stories from years' past, sharing a meal together, I could see Jesus. I could see Him on their faces, and especially in their laughter. I tucked it away. Treasuring it. Pondering it in my heart.

It only takes a moment for me to stop and treasure "these things", to ponder them in my heart, as Mary did. After all, if Mary could do it recovering from giving birth, in a barn, amongst a group of talking shepherds, couldn't I do it in my surroundings?

Let's treasure all "these things" this Christmas season, all the moments we see Jesus. Let's ponder them in our heart. Let's tuck them away. Let's take the time to be intentional about meditating on this amazing gift that God has given us. A gift that takes the punishment of our sin. A gift that grants eternal life. All we have to do is receive it.

How awesome is that?!

> "Today in the city of David there has been born for you a Savior, who is Christ the Lord." Luke 2:11

Born. For. *YOU*!!!

Drop All the Hats, Pick Up One Umbrella

We all wear a lot of hats.

This past weekend, I tried to become very overwhelmed as to just how many hats I wear. Here's just a few: mom, wife, sister, daughter, preschool director, monthly nursery volunteer, Adult Sunday School teacher, Sparks Leader (K-2nd grade), Christmas assistance family coordinator, grocery shopper, menu planner, homework helper

Since I almost had a full-on meltdown two years ago approaching Christmastime, I've learned how to balance my plate to prevent a repeat event. I truly want to celebrate this season in a manner that centers on Christ's birth. Me stressing out about all those hats is doing the opposite of what I just described.

This year, however, God and I added three things to my plate (actually, could we call it a platter?!), and I'm trying to strike a new balance. This created room---room for The Enemy to try to steal my joy.

And *that* created room for God to do His Thing in my life. (I LOVE it when God does His Thing!)

Here's what He asked of me: instead of wearing ALL those hats, why don't you drop ALL of them and pick up ONE umbrella? My umbrella--the umbrella I have over you as my child.

Drop all those hats and just be a child of God.

That sounded beautiful. It sounded freeing. It sounded wonderful. And it was! Now, I am just focusing on being God's child. Obeying Him in each step, just one step at a time.

Under His umbrella, I am protected, for He is my strong tower.
Under His umbrella, I am safe, for He is my refuge.
Under His umbrella, I am strong, for He is my strength.
Under His umbrella, I am guided, for He is my path.
Under His umbrella, I am rested, for He is my safe haven.
Under His umbrella, there are no more hats, and as much as I love to wear hats, I'm happy to drop all the ones I've been juggling.

For God's umbrella to work for me, I must *know* Him and *be known* by Him.

How can I be known by Him, if I don't talk with Him?

How can I know His direction for me, if I don't take time to listen?

If I take the time to listen, how can I know where He is leading?

To know where He is leading, I must be tuned to His voice.

How can I know His voice, if I don't read His Word?

Take the time to read God's Word, the Bible. Doing so will literally change your life. It will be an awesome transformation. Just reading the following words in my Bible provide such peace, and this is just a small morsel of the Bible! Check out these words of David found in the book of Psalm:

"Hear my cry, O God;
Give heed to my prayer.
From the end of the earth I call to You when my heart is faint;
Lead me to the rock that is higher than I.
For You have been a refuge for me,
A tower of strength against the enemy.
Let me dwell in Your tent forever;
Let me take refuge in the shelter of Your wings."
Psalm 61:1-4

Come dwell in His tent; take refuge in the shelter of His wings. Drop your hats, pick up one umbrella. Just be a child of God. Sounds pretty good, doesn't it?

What If?

What if my story, my relationship with God, my thoughts, my actions were recorded in a well-read book that people would read over and over for thousands of years?

This is what I asked myself when I was studying the book of First Samuel for my adult Sunday School Bible lesson.

Just before I posed that question to myself, I had just found myself asking aloud as I read in chapter 15, "Saul! What are you doing?! Why didn't you obey God's command all the way??? He was giving you a second chance!!!"

That's when my first question above came crashing in.

It's a sobering question.

You see, I can "yell" a question at Saul because I'm holding the entire picture in my hand. I see how the story ends. I see God's plan for him. I see God giving him a second chance at redemption. I am the reader of Saul's story, and I can see exactly where his life starts to change with the choices he makes.

What would the reader of my hypothetical story be yelling at me? The reader would have my whole life story in front of them. I can only imagine the kinds of questions the reader would have for me at different points in my life. I know that there would be extremely frustrating parts of my story that would make the reader want to pull their hair out.

But, I don't have a hypothetical reader to ponder about...I have something better. I have a relationship with the author of my story. And the amazing thing is, He actually desires this relationship with me. God knows every single part of my story because He wrote it.

I had someone ask me, "If God already knows every move, every decision that you are going to make, if He already knows where you will spend eternity, what's the point of talking to Him?"

At the time, I didn't have a response. But now, I realize that I would ask this question back, "If God already knows everything about my life, why WOULDN'T I want to talk to Him?"

When I read God's word and encounter the people that are described there, and see some of their struggles, I just want to push the pause button in time and go back to them and whisper in their ear, "God is doing this for something GOOD. Just trust in Him."

Then I think of the hypothetical reader of my hypothetical story and how they would want to do the same for me. Then it is all so clear. God has the big picture. I have a small piece of the picture.

For this reason, I will trust.

For this reason, I will obey.

Even when my small picture doesn't seem to make sense.

Because, what if my story IS being read?

What if it is being "read" in real time by others around me?

What will they see about how I trust?

What will they see about how I obey?

What will they know about my God?

What if?

Lord, I pray that when others see me, that they will see You. Humble me, so I can get myself out of the way for you to work. Father, forgive me when I put myself, my thoughts, my actions before Yours. Help me to walk step-by-step in the path You have forged for me. Thank you for authoring my story, but even more, thank you for the relationship we have. For You know, that I could not do this life on my own strength. I need You with every step I make and every breath I breathe, and I thank you for always being there. Lord, You are amazing. Please keep me continually amazed by You.

A Deep Question

On our way home from my parents' house on Christmas Evening, we had just hit the highway, and the hum of the tires on the road helped us settle into the ride ahead. The dogs had found their perfect spots--one on the floor of the car, and the other in the seat with our daughter. When out of the clear blue night sky, our son asks us,

"How do I deepen my relationship with God?"

Wow! What a deep question for our newly 11-year-old!

I replied, "Wow, son, God must be knocking on your heart wanting you to get to know Him better. The way to do that is to spend time with Him...reading the Bible and talking with Him through prayer. That's so very cool that you are sensitive to the Spirit nudging you."

Our son can at times be a guy of few words, (not all the time, mind you, at church his new nickname is "Gabby", since he doesn't stop talking) and this was one of those few-word times. He just hummed a "Hmmm" response and looked out the window.

Brandon turned the radio volume back up, and we rocked on with our ride. A few minutes later, our son asked Brandon, "could you please turn down the radio, it keeps interrupting my thoughts about God, and I just want to think about Him for a while?"

Well, absolutely, little buddy! We turned down the radio & rode the rest of the way in a comfortable silence, allowing him to meditate on God.

That night, instead of reading his new Star Wars books in bed, he read in his Bible.

The next morning when he woke up, he read in his Bible, instead of heading straight for the Xbox.

The next night at bedtime, he reached again for his Bible.

Let me pause here to tell you that our kids LOVE to read. We are those parents who have to scold them to put down the book at the dinner table, when someone is talking to them, while walking in a parking lot, at bedtime, etc. As soon as the twins were old enough to walk, we started going to the library weekly and still haven't stopped. (This is a mystery to Brandon, who could take or leave a library!)

Okay, so it's bedtime and our son has his Bible open reading away. After tucking them in and saying prayers, Brandon & I stood out in the hallway pondering what to do. How do you tell a child to close his Bible & go to bed??? You don't. I told Brandon, "I'm not telling him to close his Bible." So we walked away & let the Holy Spirit do His thing!

This morning, I was already up spending time with God, drinking my coffee, when I heard our son wake up. Normally, I hear his door open, then moments later I'll hear the toilet flush, then I hear the playroom door close, which means he has gone in there to play the Xbox and he closes the door so as to not wake his sister. Today, however, I hear his door open, moments later I hear the toilet flush, then I hear him bounce back into his bed, with the sound of the pages of the Bible turning to find where he left off the night before.

It was such a beautiful sound. There is just something so special about hearing those onion-skin pages turning. I loved it!

I sat there and marveled at the mighty work of the Holy Spirit. You see, our son's thirst for God's word did not come from me or Brandon, it came from the Holy Spirit. If us, as his parents, would have told him, you need to read your Bible when you lay down and when you wake up, it wouldn't have stuck with him like this. The only thing we can do as parents, is pray for him and his journey with Christ, model what the relationship looks like, train him up in the ways of the Lord, and then step back and let the Holy Spirit do His thing!

This all started with him being sensitive to a question planted by the Holy Spirit:

"How can I deepen my relationship with God?"

Deepen. When I thought of that word, I could only come up with positive connotations:

Dig deep.

Go deep. (Like on a football field.)

Deep sea fishing.

To deepen is a good thing. Let's do it. Let's go deep with Christ. Let's be sensitive to the stirring of the Holy Spirit when He wants us to take our relationship with Christ deeper than before. Let's pray for a renewed thirst for God's word. Let's fill the quiet with the sound of onion-skin pages of Bibles turning, soaking in the Word of God. What a beautiful sound it is!

Sweat and Sisters

There's nothing like a good workout to release stress on the body. I recently encountered a new term for sweat and I love it....here it is: "I'm not sweating, that's my body crying." Isn't that great?! I love workouts that make my body cry!

A few years ago, I started running as a way to release stress, to have some "me" time, which also doubled as "girl time", since I would run with a partner. However, I kept losing my running partners. They moved away...like really far away! I live in the southeastern part of the US, and my running parters moved to California, then Texas, and then I *walked* with my neighbor, and she moved to upstate New York! Since running alone was just not the same, I tried out Jazzercise and I instantly loved it!

I know, I know, a one-piece full-body, belted leotard just flashed through your head, didn't it? If it did, that's okay, it won't change my stance of my love for Jazzercise.

I have to tell you what happened one night at Jazzercise. I have several acquaintances in class, and we'll do a little small talk before class. There's one lady named Rhonda that just shines. She always has a smile and an easy laugh. She's one of those people that just make you feel better by just being near her. I don't know a whole lot about her, but we have established that we are sisters in Christ. It was one of those things you could just sense, you know?

This particular night, after the cardio portion, we headed to get our free weights off the rack to enter into the weight portion of the workout, and when we passed, I told Rhonda "hey", and she asked, "how are you?", and I said, "I'm fine". All seems like simple chit-chat while we were quickly transitioning, right? Wrong. Being a sister in the faith, she knew I wasn't right. And she *was* right. The sweat had not exactly shaken all the stress off just yet. She immediately asked, "Do you need me to pray for you?".

Um, yes please! Like all the time! I don't know that there's a moment that goes by that I don't need someone praying for me. I'm a bona-fide mess! Without Christ, without prayers, I'd NEVER be able to get through a day.

I told her that I would love that and that we could catch up later. Then, with the workout gearing back up, we parted ways.

During the weights routines, I thought so much about that very brief encounter. I wonder all the time how people who do not have a community of faith even get through this thing called life.

The sweat didn't take my stress tonight, but my sister-in-Christ did. And for her, I'm so grateful. She "said" more to me in that brief encounter than she will ever know. Just knowing someone is praying for you is such a powerful thing. For our battles are not against flesh and blood, but rather against the forces of darkness, against evil. Prayer combats this, and it's a widely unused tool in this battle.

Let's gear up, sisters and brothers in Christ. We've got a battle to fight.

Lord, thank you so much for placing encouragers in our paths at just at the right time. Thank you for faithful prayer warriors. Thank you for my sister-in-Christ tonight who just "knew". Lord, help me to be an encourager, as she encouraged me. Please give me your eyes to see when there is someone in need of prayer, someone that needs lifting up, someone that needs more of You. Father, for those that don't have a community of faith, I pray that you will lead them to one. Lead them by just the right person in just the right moment, and let them be uninhibited to receive You. Let them ask, and then, Lord, equip us with the words to say, Your words, not ours, so that they can come to know You too, and have this awesome community of faith that has been such a gift to me. In Jesus name I pray, Amen.

"For our struggle is not against flesh and blood, but against the rulers, against the powers, against the world forces of this darkness, against the spiritual forces of wickedness in the heavenly places." Ephesians 6:12

A Wooden Bowl

Last Spring, I went through a season where I was feeling very overwhelmed. It just all seemed too much.

My husband and I teach an adult Sunday School class (aka "a small group"). During the prayer request share time, I don't usually share about me, but this time I did. I asked for prayer, because my platter (not my plate) felt so full. PLEASE do not see this as complaining, but rather more of an explanation (it came across okay in person, but I want to make sure it comes across in written form)---I mentioned about all the people I was carrying on my platter: the 92 preschoolers and their families that are a part of the preschool where I'm the director, the thirteen ladies I have on preschool staff, my 25 kindergarten-2nd graders I teach on Wednesday nights, and the 25 members of our Sunday School class. I want to be able to pour into all these precious people that God has brought into my life, but at this particular point, I was feeling so overwhelmed that I couldn't even get complete sentences from my mind to my mouth correctly. I had fumbled through the previous Sunday School lesson; I just couldn't get my thoughts and words to line up correctly. There was just too much going on in my head to be able to even think right.

A few moments later during the class, Sunshine, a gal in our class, had a vision that was just burning in her heart and needed to be shared. Her vision was related to the prayer request I had shared, and in her vision she saw a beautiful, long banquet table, set with several place settings of china. Fragile, eloquent china, complete with those itty-bitty china tea cups that hardly hold a spot of tea. It was in those dainty dishes that I was trying to put everything, which obviously, wasn't working, since they hardly held anything. Then she described a smaller table that was next to this grandiose one. This table just had one place setting. A simple place setting, all made of wood. A carpenter's place setting. Jesus' place setting. This place setting had no bottom. It could hold EVERYTHING. Everything that "my platter" couldn't. All I needed was to place everything that was on my platter onto this wooden place setting, giving it all to Jesus.

The Wednesday prior to this particular Sunday, Al, a gentleman in our class, had brought a wooden bowl that he had made that week to church. Al is an incredible wood-worker, and his creations are literally breath-taking. I had held the bowl that he made, admiring it, and remarked about how smooth it was, how detailed it was. His wooden creations usually have a story to go with them, and Al can tell you exactly what kind of tree it was made from, and even where he encountered the tree.

I am a visual learner, and it's how I get things to stick in my mind, so after Sunshine shared her vision, I had told the class about Al's bowl and how I was going to picture that bowl whenever my platter feels full, and I would figuratively, put everything I'm carrying in the Carpenter's bowl, leaving it with Jesus.

The next week during class, Al, and his lovely wife Judi, presented me with a bowl Al had made for me. It was made from a cherry tree, and is such a priceless gift, a precious keepsake that comes with such a beautiful reminder of how our Savior wants us to cast our cares on Him, because He cares for us.

There's room in the Carpenter's wooden bowl for your cares too. All we have to do is trust God with our lives, our cares, our burdens, then seek Him in all our ways, acknowledge Him in all we do, and He will direct our path.

"Cast all your anxiety on Him, because He cares for you."   1 Peter 5:7

"Trust in the LORD with all your heart And do not lean on your own understanding. In all your ways acknowledge Him, And He will make your paths straight."   Proverbs 3:5-6

But God Causes the Growth

There is so much to unpack in the beginning of First Corinthians 3. But, man oh man, have I been completely struck with five words:

But. God. Causes. The. Growth.

How dare I even think for one nano-second that I,...me,...Carly, can give someone the faith to believe. This is for God alone. Only He can cause the growth.

The weather this week has literally drawn me out of my house. I just cannot get enough of the outdoors lately. I love to read outside, but even when I wanted a break from reading, I didn't want to go inside, so I've been doing things I have literally NEVER done on my own....get ready....I hope some of you who know me well are sitting down....here goes:

I've been working outside. Like yard work. Like getting dirty. Like dirt has been under my fingernails. AND I LOVE IT!

While spending so much time outside, I've noticed all the buds on trees literally ready to burst forth. While I'm not looking forward to the onslaught of the pollen attack that comes with those buds opening, I am ready to see their beauty.

But, I can no more go to those tree

limbs and open those buds myself than I can give a person the faith he/she needs to believe in the Lord Jesus Christ as Savior.

Only God can do both of these things.
Only God causes the growth.
Not me.
Not a Sunday School Class.
Not an amazing message.
Not a conversation.
Not works.
Only God.

I can plant. Another can water. But it is God who causes the growth.

Lord, keep me humble. Thank you for this reminder. How dare I think that I am anything without You. You, alone, are the One who causes the growth. You give opportunity to me, and I pray that I am found faithful with what/whom You have entrusted me with. Lord, keep my eyes fixed on the fact that I am Your fellow worker, Your field, Your building. And nothing more. All I am, all I have, belongs to You, and only You cause the growth. Keep my heart broken for those whom have not found faith in You. For it is in You that I find life, and it is this life that I desire for others to discover too. Amen.

"What then is Apollos? And what is Paul? Servants through whom you believed, even as the Lord gave *opportunity* to each one. I planted, Apollos watered, but God was causing the growth. So then neither the one who plants nor the one who waters is anything, but God who causes the growth. Now he who plants and he who waters are one; but each will receive his own reward according to his own labor. For we are God's fellow workers; you are God's field, God's building."
1 Corinthians 3:5-9

Looking 20 Years Younger for the Sake of Sharing Jesus

So, this moment happened one morning that totally made a parable come to life for me. I'm SO thankful that this moment was shared with a friend of mine, because it's pretty crazy, and she was there to prove it was all real!

My friend, Marie, and I went to Chick-fil-A one morning for breakfast to share and encourage one another about what God is doing in our lives. We had a really awesome time together. I just LOVE hearing about how God is moving and celebrating together where we have each seen Him.

So, we had wrapped up and were heading to my car, when a man in his late 70's asked from behind us, "So, when's finals?"

We live in a college town. (It's actually a really awesome college town in Athens, Georgia, where the University of Georgia is located.)

We laughed, and Marie told him that we were old, which caused him to return the laugh with a scoff. Since he was so skeptical and swore that we were freshman co-eds, we told him our ages, which shocked him. If he only knew how much more shocking the conversation was about to be....

As he was still scoffing and turning to leave, I asked him how old he was. (It was only fair, right?! I mean, we had just disclosed our ages!)

He didn't seem to like this question too much, so he just threw a look back at me.

Noticing his UGA trucker hat, his large presence, and his watch with the unmistakable "G" for Georgia, I asked him if he was affiliated with UGA.

This peeked his interest, he turned back toward us, and launched into an interesting conversation about how he is a retired Agriculture Professor from UGA, and for the next several minutes, he told us details about his financial retirement, and how he was thankful for increases in his retirement in years when teachers were otherwise not getting raises, about how he is able to draw a double-retirement, and on and on and on.

It was during his description of his retirement that "it" happened. That roller-coaster-like gut-drop that happens when I feel the Holy Spirit prompting me to share.

Thankfully, it was also this same moment that Marie asked him, "So, you don't have to worry about money at all, do you?"

I was thankful for this stall, because I had to send up a quick prayer for guidance. I got no impression that this man really *knew* Jesus, so I had the feeling it could get interesting.

He answered Marie's question with, "You know, actually, I don't."

Wow.

So, here goes.....I asked him, "So it sounds like your earthly retirement is secure, how about your eternal retirement?"

Since he was taller than me, he dips his head even lower, and says, "What?"

"Your eternal retirement?"

Blank stare back.

So I asked, "Do you know Jesus?" There it was. The bomb-like effect of the name of Jesus.

He scoffed. And turned to go, saying that he had to get to the bank.

Cause, that's where his hope is, you know?

He paused and turned back. Thankfully, because I didn't want it to end there, he launched into a conversation about my car. He asked me if I enjoyed driving it. I told him that I did, and that is was a secure ride (it was my intention to try to turn this conversation back to Jesus, since He's my secure ride to heaven---see what I was doing there?).

After the car chit-chat, I pointed to the large, white roof of our church that could be seen from where we were. I asked him, "Do you see that large, white roof?"

He said, "Yes."

Reaching into my purse to grab my church business card, I said, "That's where I work. Here's my card. I'd love to talk to you more about Jesus, if you would like."

Shocking me by accepting my card (I truly thought he would reject it), he shared a light smile, or maybe it was just his lip twitching, and he turned to walk to his car.

When Marie and I got into my car, we didn't know whether to think that encounter was awkward or awesome, but either way, we loved it!

We talked about how it was just SO COOL that God used two girls that He loves to plant a seed into the heart of a man that He loves too!

I told Marie that, knowing God, I wouldn't doubt it for one second that God will use someone to water that seed soon.

Perhaps while at the bank, God used someone else to share Jesus. Or, maybe He'll use the sunset tonight to show this man just how majestic and wonderful our Creator is. Either way, we both felt loved, wonderful, excited to be used by God to plant that little seed. Which goes right with the previous story about how God causes the growth.

Pretty fitting for a retired agriculture professor, right?

Also? It's just too cool that God made us appear as young as "freshman co-eds" to plant a seed. At the time, that was 19 years ago for me; and let's face it, that's a miracle right there!!!

The Parable of the Rich Young Ruler:

"And someone came to Him and said, "Teacher, what good thing shall I do that I may obtain eternal life?" And He said to him, "Why are you asking Me about what is good? There is *only* One who is good; but if you wish to enter into life, keep the commandments." *Then* he said to Him, "Which ones?" And Jesus said, "You shall not commit murder; You shall not commit adultery; You shall not steal; You shall not bear false witness; Honor your father and mother; and You shall love your neighbor as yourself." The young man said to Him, "All these things I have kept; what am I still lacking?" Jesus said to him, "If you wish to be complete, go *and* sell your possessions and give to *the* poor, and you will have treasure in heaven; and come, follow Me." But when the young man heard this statement, he went away grieving; for he was one who owned much property.

And Jesus said to His disciples, "Truly I say to you, it is hard for a rich man to enter the kingdom of heaven. Again I say to you, it is easier for a camel to go through the eye of a needle, than for a rich man to enter the kingdom of God." When the disciples heard *this*, they were very astonished and said,

"Then who can be saved?" And looking at *them* Jesus said to them, "With people this is impossible, but with God all things are possible.""
Matthew 19:16-26

More Jesus

At the Good Friday service at our church, we had communion. Communion at my church consists of those teeny-tiny little plastic cups filled with grape juice and tiny wafers about the size of a quarter. (The grape juice represents the blood of Christ; the wafers, His body.) Sitting near me was a little girl, whom when the tray of little grape juice cups and tiny wafers were passed by her, she helped herself to several of those little wafers.

While her mama was trying to correct her that she's only to take one, I couldn't help the smile that formed across my face.

Now, let me be clear....had it been my child to take several wafers, I would've done the exact same thing as this mama, but since it *wasn't* my child, I was left to enjoy the imagery this moment brought.

She just wanted more Jesus.

I mean, let's face it, in children's church, our kiddos are taught about just how wonderful Jesus is and how even more wonderful, was what He did for us on the cross---taking the punishment for our sins. So, why wouldn't we expect that when the children join us for a family communion service, that they wouldn't want to soak up more Jesus?!?!

Being honest, I had such great intentions about slowing down approaching this holy week. Taking the time to reflect, to ponder, to meditate on all aspects of this Easter season and exactly what it means. Unfortunately, instead, life revved up around me. While I still was able to spend time with God each day, it wasn't the slow-down I was hoping for.

BUT...the imagery that this girl provided has totally blessed my heart. More Jesus. Grabbing up as much of Him as I can in every moment.

For, He knows the desires of my heart. And, my desires would be to do just as that sweet girl did....soak up as much of Jesus as I possibly can!

"Delight yourself in the LORD; And He will give you the desires of your heart."
Psalm 37:4

"While they were eating, Jesus took *some* bread, and after a blessing, He broke *it* and gave *it* to the disciples, and said, "Take, eat; this is My body." And when He had taken a cup and given thanks, He gave *it* to them, saying, "Drink from it, all of you; for this is My blood of the covenant, which is poured out for many for forgiveness of sins. But I say to you, I will not drink of this fruit of the vine from now on until that day when I drink it new with you in My Father's kingdom.""
Matthew 26:26-29

Listen to the Birds

One day I was pulling out of my neighborhood to go to work, while my neighbor, who is retired, was taking a walk. I was actually running a little bit early (shocker, I know), so I stopped and rolled down my window for a quick chat.

He told me that he was having some tests done that day to see about the diagnosis of an enlarged heart. He had told me that he was a bit anxious about it. Listening to the birds that were totally signing to us that morning, I told him that when I am anxious about something, I listen to the birds and think of the verse that says:

"For this reason I say to you, do not be worried about your life, *as to* what you will eat or what you will drink; nor for your body, *as to* what you will put on. Is not life more than food, and the body more than clothing? Look at the birds of the air, that they do not sow, nor reap nor gather into barns, and *yet* your heavenly Father feeds them. Are you not worth much more than they? And who of you by being worried can add a *single* hour to his life?"
Matthew 6:25-27

Look at the birds. God totally provides for them.

Hearing the birds, I can remember this command that Jesus spoke to not worry.

I told him that I would be praying for him, and that while he finished his walk, to just listen to the birds.

Little did I know that I would need this very same advice for myself just a few short hours later.

Nine days before this particular day, I had changed up the way I had been praying for my dad's recovery from his massive stroke 16 years ago. I started praying that my dad's life would be rescued from the pit that was narcotic drug use for pain relief. You see, his doctor had chosen to manage his pain in this manner for the past 9 years. This put my dad in a viscous cycle of sleep, wake up to take meds, go back to sleep. There was not a whole lot more to this daily routine, which had been troubling me greatly, hence the change in prayer.

Things had been building in the past two weeks, as my dad was trying out ways to get more. More pain killers, and not just oral meds, but going to the hospital for IV meds. This was not him. This was addiction. I could not understand how a doctor could keep writing this prescription month after month after month for nine long years.

I encouraged my mom to get a plan in place. I knew that something had to give.

It was on this same day that I had encouraged my sweet neighbor to listen to the birds, that my dad had tried another "stunt" to get more. My mom called me to let me know that she and my dad were both ready for the help that is rehab. Within a very short span of time, he was packed and admitted into a rehab facility by that afternoon.

This is a hard thing, especially since the initial phase is being cut-off from the world, and since my dad has stroke-induced aphasia, he could not effectively communicate what he was going through when we were able to talk to him.

I had to trust strangers to my dad's care.

I had to trust that he didn't feel alone or abandoned.

I had to listen to the birds.

This happening was an answer to my prayer, but it is the very beginning of a long road. So, I've got to trust God. God already knew what that day held for me. For my mom. For my dad. This turn of events did not take Him by surprise. And, is my dad not worth much more than the birds?

God will take care of him.
God will take care of my mom.
God will take care of me.
God will take care of you.
We've just got to trust Him to do so.

And my neighbor? His test results showed no enlarged heart. Praise be to God!

Do *you* hear the birds?

Lord, You are an amazing provider. You take care of the birds, who do not sow, reap, or gather into barns. How much more will you take care of us? Lord, please keep me from worrying by helping me to remember this promise. You let me know over and over in Your Word, that if I call to you, come to You and pray, that You will listen to me. I will seek and find You when I search for You with all my heart. (Jer. 29: 12-13) Lord, take my whole heart. Take my life. For this is my offering. It's all I have to give, and it's all Yours. Amen.

The Nod

The first time I took a ride in my husband's 1995 Jeep Wrangler, I learned something I never knew before...

We were riding along and as we passed a driver going the opposite direction, my husband, Brandon, threw up a wave, of sorts. (It was more like a few fingers extended from the steering wheel combined with a nod.)

So, I asked him, "Do you know that guy?"

"Nope."

Okay then.

Then, a while later, the same encounter happened. Only this time, I put two and two together...it was a secret club of sorts....a wave only shared by fellow Jeep owners...it was the "Jeep Wave".

This was so cool to me! It was like a big 'ole support system out there on the open road. It's like, "Hey! What's Up! Oh, you're a fellow jeep-driver? Rock on brother!"

It just made me smile so big.

It was just a gesture acknowledging that you have something in common, and I was fascinated by it! I started looking for fellow "jeepers", just to get ready to witness "the wave".

I'm a dork. I know.

This does not only happen for Jeep-drivers, it is also out there for motorcycles too. Their wave is a bit different; they put out a couple fingers down low and out to the side.

Here's the thing though...the only way you can experience either of these is to get in the Jeep. Or take a ride on a motorcycle. You can't experience this particular band of brotherhood any other way.

Then, I got to thinking. A dangerous place sometimes, I know. Here goes....bear with me.....joining a body of fellow believers in Jesus is a way of experiencing the "What's up" nod. When I walk through the hallways of my local church, I get to throw a smile, a nod, a hug, a "what's up". It's like saying, "Hey there, sister! How are you? You carrying your cross too? Right on! We can do this! Just another few days in the world till we meet up here again!" It's like a band of brotherhood/ sisterhood with other Jesus-followers with whom I have something in common. It's like a big 'ole support system that I can tap into twice weekly (and sometimes even more than that).

Here's the thing though...the only way you can experience this type of support system is to get in the door and join up with a group. If you are not a part of a fellow body of believers, I encourage you to find one. For me, it's my local church, but I know that it's different for others. Either way, it's a great thing to be with fellow Jesus-followers to share that common bond and have fellowship together.

Side note: there is not a nod for the particular SUV I drive. I know because I tried.

What is God's Will Concerning Me?

Have you ever asked this question before? God's will involves three actions. Not everyone is going to like hearing these three actions, because two of them require a good helping of faith.

Also, I believe that we get better and better at these three things the longer and closer that we walk with God. So, take hope if you are a new follower of Jesus---this will get easier!

Here you go....

God's Will:
1. Rejoice always
2. Pray without ceasing
3. In everything give thanks

See? I told you two of these would be hard.

Rejoice always. Besides the obvious hardships we encounter in life, do you want to know where I have the hardest time rejoicing? In traffic. Yep, sitting parked in traffic. It drives me batty. Thank goodness I live in a rural area, so traffic is not a part of my daily life, but when I have been sitting in traffic, it is so very hard to rejoice.

The "pray without ceasing" part comes easy for me, because I need prayer to get through every moment of my day! It's like a constant stream of communication that never ends.

In everything give thanks. I attended a prayer conference a few months ago, where I was challenged to take the worst thing that has happened in my life and thank God for it.

Wait, what?

I did not understand at the time, but I trusted and did it. I thanked God for my dad's stroke. My dad's stroke was massive and it radically changed his life. And I thanked God for it??? This seemed so very wrong on every level.

But what it did in my heart was amazing.

Thanking God for this event was another way of putting my faith into action. This gesture shows God that I trust Him, even though I don't understand why some things happen. And thanking Him made a piece of bitterness that I was harboring in my heart fall away.

If you choose to follow God's will for your life, some of you will thank God for losing a loved one. For being laid off from a job. For cancer. For watching someone suffer with illness. For losing a child.

How do we muster the energy, the ability, to do this? Where would that come from?

Not from us, for sure! It would be the Holy Spirit at work in us.

I know how crazy this sounds. Believe me. When I sat in that prayer conference, I thought the speaker had lost his mind.

But....

It really is amazing when you have the faith to thank God for the valley you are currently in, or for a valley that you have already been through. I couldn't put into words to describe what it does, so you're just going to have to trust me on this one.

Correction, don't trust my words.....trust God's Word....."Rejoice always; pray without ceasing; in everything give thanks; for this is God's will for you in Christ Jesus." 1 Thessalonians 5:28

There's a Devotion Book on My Trashcan

There's a devotion book on the trashcan in my garage.

That's a very strange place for a devotion book, isn't it?!

The reason it is there is because of the following passage in the Bible:

"You shall therefore impress these words of mine on your heart and on your soul; and you shall bind them as a sign on your hand, and they shall be as frontals on your forehead. You shall teach them to your sons, talking of them when you sit in your house and when you walk along the road and when you lie down and when you rise up. You shall write them on the doorposts of your house and on your gates..."
Deuteronomy 11:18-20

In this passage, God is enlightening the Israelites as to what they should do with their knowledge of Him, and that is to SHARE IT. God desires that the act of sharing about Him is so wonderful, and necessary, that it becomes a part of our daily lives. He also designates that it should be shared with our children, meaning those in the generation behind us.

That's why there's a devotion book--in

my garage--on a trashcan.

Let me explain--last year, we drove our twins to school, so we had the devotion book in our car to be read aloud on the way to school. Following the reading, we took turns praying over our day. Now, the twins ride the bus to school in the morning. So, we wait by the garage.

You see where this is going, don't you?

I've learned the hard way about placing objects on my car's bumper. I drove all the way to our veterinarian's office with our cordless phone on the bumper. Anyone who knows my style of driving, knows that it's a bon-a-fide miracle that phone was still on the bumper when we got home. (I didn't notice it until the next time the home phone rang, which is rare these days.)

So, since the bumper is not a safe place, and I didn't want it to be on the ground, the trashcan it is. The point is, set yourself up for success. Place God's Word or devotion books where they can be utilized in opportune moments. As a young family, if we are to teach our children when we sit, when we walk by the way, when we lie down, when we get up, and might I add, when we wait for the school bus, then this is how we do it.

One day, following the reading of that days' particular devotion, my daughter said that she's glad we have this routine, because there was an event in her day the day prior where she was able to draw comfort from the words we read that morning, which described an attribute of our loving God who cares for us.

I would encourage you to incorporate this idea into your daily routine and to set yourself up for success for conversations about Jesus. If that book was not at arm's reach at the bus stop, I can attest that reading it wouldn't happen. Reading scripture is a great way to begin a morning prayer time, and what better way for my kids to begin their school day, literally steps before loading the bus, than spending time with Jesus?

As Yourself

My husband, Brandon, taught me a love lesson when I saw his belt, socks, wallet and watch laid out on his bathroom counter one night. Brandon lays these items out every Thursday night, so I'm used to seeing them then, but seeing them on a Monday night made me take pause to notice them.

On Friday mornings, Brandon leaves before I wake up to meet with men from our church for a time of weekly prayer and encouragement. This morning, he had to lead a training at work at 5:30am, so he was "up and at 'em" before I woke up.

He sets those items out on his bathroom counter, because they normally live in our bedroom, and to see them, he would have to turn on the light, or rummage around in the dark, either of which, would wake me.

Love.

A gesture that is truly loving another as yourself. Which is exactly how Jesus wants us to love.

"'Teacher, which is the great commandment in the Law?' And He said to him, 'You shall love the Lord your God with all your heart, and with all your soul, and with all your mind.' This is the great and foremost

commandment. The second is like it, 'You shall love your neighbor as yourself.'"
Matthew 22:35-39

When I saw these items on the bathroom counter last night, it made my heart swell, and I praised God for picking out THE MOST amazing husband for me.

Not only did this most selfless gesture made me praise God, it also inspired/encouraged/motivated me to look for ways where I could love others the way that Brandon loves me, which is ultimately the way that God loves us.

Could you imagine a world where we loved others like we love ourselves? Where God's love is the example, not the exception? Where we put others first?

Could you imagine a workplace where this happens?

Could you imagine a home where this happens?

Let's not imagine. Let's just do it. You know, look for ways where we could put others first. Look for ways to love as Jesus loves. Love the Lord our God with ALL our hearts, souls, minds, and then love the ones around us as ourselves.

Because when we do, we point others to the love of Christ. And that's what we are here for anyways, right?

Thank you, Brandon, for loving me as Christ loves His church. You inspire me. I love you so much.

Dogs and Dumplings

Last week I fed my dogs made-from-scratch Chicken and Dumplings.

Oh, this was not the intention of the meal, but it was the result of the leftovers.

I LOVE Chicken and Dumplings. I fell in love with them several years ago one summer when we were doing a lot of traveling. When the fast food got old, it was Cracker Barrel all the way. Those Chicken and Dumplings called to me from the highway!

I also LOVE to cook and I enjoy trying new recipes. I'm a couponer and I make our menu for the week based on what's on sale. So, when the whole chickens were on sale...you guessed it.... Chicken and Dumplings time!

I found an old-fashioned recipe and did EVERYTHING from scratch. I didn't even use canned chicken broth! I cooked the chicken whole, and made the homemade dough for the dumplings, cutting the dough into individual dumplings, before they were cooked in the homemade broth.

Don't get me wrong, my family and I were able to enjoy this meal. But, you have to understand that I LOVE leftover night almost more than I love chocolate. I call leftover night "Mom's Buffet", which is wording I stole from a friend of mine.

All the taste.

None of the work.

You just heat up all those Tupperwares from the fridge, lay them out on the kitchen counter, and have your family go through the "buffet" line. It's an amazing thing. Truly. And my people love it!

But I digress.

So, the next morning after this goodness was cooked, I went out to the garage where the dog food bin is stored to fill the dog bowls for their meal.

Ants, ants, and more ants were everywhere. Like. every. where.

Since the dog food bin was nearly empty, we had bought a new bag at the grocery store the night before. I was so grateful for this, since there was NO WAY I could feed my four-legged babies food that was covered in ants.

You guessed it...the ants had found a way into that brand-new bag of food. I was sick to my stomach. That discovery was like throwing money straight into the trash.

I couldn't let these precious beings go hungry. This was a Sunday morning, where there is never any extra time in the routine to make a run to the store, so I racked my brain about the most mild food we had on hand, to not upset their delicate stomachs.

(Translation: I didn't want to come home to doggie messes made by upset stomachs.)

Yep, you guessed right again...the Chicken and Dumplings. Those little pieces of goodness went straight into the dog bowls. Where they lasted exactly ten seconds.

You guys, they didn't even savor the love that went into that meal! They didn't take pause to look at me with grateful eyes. Those little rascals devoured them exactly like they devour their dry, tasteless dog food! At least my family had the decency to rave the night before when they were eating that meal made with so much love.

Now I know why there is no sense in feeding our animals 5 Star cuisine. They wouldn't know the difference from a fast food cheeseburger and a steak from a 5 Star restaurant. It really doesn't matter to them because they are unaware as to what they are missing out on.

Experiencing my dogs' total lack of appreciation for my made-from-scratch dumplings made this message from Jesus come alive for me:

"Do not give what is holy to dogs, and do not throw your pearls before swine, or they will trample them under their feet, and turn and tear you to pieces."
Matthew 7:6

People who are hostile to the message

of the saving gospel of Jesus Christ, do not know what they are missing, therefore, are not ready to hear it. This fact proves to be troublesome to my "fix-it" personality, and my desire to broadcast to everyone I encounter the Good News of Jesus---that He died for US, and that He is SO WORTH knowing.

This is why it is SO important for me to not make ONE STEP ahead of the Holy Spirit. For, when I do, it's like giving dumplings to dogs, or in Jesus' example, pearls to pigs.

Seeing my sweet, precious dogs not enjoy all the energy I put into making those dumplings was heart-breaking. Just as I'm sure it's heart-breaking to my Savior watching me put way too much time and energy into someone/something who/that is just not ready to receive Him. For, He knows just the right timing, and He'll let me know when He's ready for me to pour into someone, or spend time on a project/event.

It's a waste to make "dumplings for dogs" and to throw "pearls before pigs". These are the things that distract us, or keep us busy, from doing what the Lord actually wants us to do. And goodness knows we need to cut out as much busywork as we can!

Let's evaluate the things that are keeping us busy and make sure that they are in line with what God would have us do during this season in our lives. Perhaps we are working ourselves to the bone trying to make something happen, where if we would just put those things down, and instead pick-up what God would have us pick-up, our garden of effort would burst forth in soil that has already been tilled by the Holy Spirit!

And, that, my friends, is where our "dumplings" would be savored!

A Blue Bead

One Friday, I was having a rough start to my morning, which started the evening before.

There's seven roles I try to fulfill each day:
Wife
Mom
Preschool Director
Housekeeper/Chef
Exercise partaker
Me time
God time

I know you may be thinking, why doesn't "exercise partaker" fall under "me time"? That's a great question. It's because going to Jazzercise class and sitting on the couch eating Moose Tracks ice cream and Lay's plain potato chips while watching a prerecorded House Hunters show is on totally different ends of the spectrum!

Each day no matter how hard I try, I've never been able to fulfill all seven roles. Something always gives.

On Thursday night, the "mom" role gave. My 6th grade daughter, who is SO responsible, gave me a school form on Monday that was due on Friday.

Thursday night it was absolutely necessary for me to make it to Jazzercise class. The stress from the week was taking a toll, and several circumstances prevented me from working out the week before. So, I was going on almost two weeks without a workout, which meant my back was feeling the strain.

I made Jazzercise a priority that evening, which meant the "mom" role gave, and the form didn't get filled out.

I realized this fact Friday morning on the way into work.

This was all on me. It was my fault, as she had done her part.

Picturing my daughter with tears welling up, spilling out of her sensitive heart and into her eyes when she arrived in 5th period without the form, I called my husband to see if he could help me think through a rational, logical plan to get this to her at school, since I was coming up blank.

Brandon (my husband) told me he would take care of it. This was not the plan that I wanted, as it wasn't him who forgot, but I must admit, I breathed a huge sigh of relief.

He had arrived at home and had FaceTimed me to help him find where I left the form, at the same time that the sweet, sweet children, who are enrolled in the preschool where I work, started arriving for school that day.

I was tucked inside an empty

classroom trying to sort out my short-coming via FaceTime, when Annie, a four-year-old, brought me a gift.

A blue bead.

I asked if I could hug her, and she agreed. She, nor her mom, knows how much this gesture meant to me during a time when I was trying to be very hard on myself.

Good grief, I have tears welling up now just recounting this!

I kept that bead in my pocket all day. Each time I felt of it, I smiled. My heart warmed. It brought such a warm feeling over me...a feeling of being loved just as I am, even when I make mistakes.

Did I *NEED* a blue bead? Nope. I wasn't planning on making a bracelet or craft with beads.

Did I appreciate the blue bead? You betcha!

Does God *NEED* our gifts? Nope.
Does He appreciate them? You betcha!

When we give God our praise, money, time, and talents, it lets Him know how much we love Him, how grateful we are to Him. It's the very thought of our gifts that reflects what is in our hearts.

Our generosity also changes those around us. Annie totally changed up my day with her blue bead gift. (And actually, since time has passed and this bead still makes me smile, Annie's generosity is a gift that will keep on giving.)

Love God. Love others. Change the hearts around you by doing so.

If a four-year-old can do it, what's stopping me? What's stopping you?

"Teacher, which is the great commandment in the Law?" And He said to him, "'You shall love the Lord your God with all your heart, and with all your soul, and with all your mind.' This is the great and foremost commandment. The second is like it, 'You shall love your neighbor as yourself.' On these two commandments depend the whole Law and the Prophets."
Matthew 22:36-40

When Coffee Attacks

The events in this story that you are about to read are completely 100% true.

Each Friday afternoon, I set up the room where my husband, Brandon, and I teach Sunday School. The room where we teach is a multi-use room, so it must be broken-down and set up each week. This is actually a good thing, because while I am setting up the seven tables and 32 chairs, I'm praying. I pray over our class as a whole, over each of the people whom attend our class, over the people yet to join our class, for God to keep Brandon and I broken, humble, poured-out, so God can be strong through us, and give us the words to say each week, etc. However, this past Friday had unexpected events, so I did not have time to do so.

My family was at the church building on Saturday, so we set up the room then, but because our favorite college football team was about to kickoff, we didn't take the time to pray over the class as usual. (Lord, forgive us!)

So, on Sunday morning, I told Brandon that I was going to watch the sunrise on the back porch and pray over the class. Now, you need to know that I have an extreme, warranted fear of spiders (that's a story for another day), so I told him that if I encountered "an unmentionable" while sitting in the dark awaiting the sunrise, that I would wake the entire neighborhood.

A short spell later, Brandon joined me. I told him that I was praying with my eyes open, so I didn't miss the sunrise, so he should too. So, we took turns praying, and when we finished, we sat there chatting, finishing our coffee, awaiting the sun to fully wake up the day, as it was still a bit dark. Little did we know that there would indeed be yelling, but it would not be caused by "an unmentionable".

Now, here's where you need to bear with me, as it's going to be hard to explain this next segment. I wish so badly there was a video of this next part, because I would watch it on repeat!

Okay, so remember, it's still dark, and we have coffee with us.

All of the sudden, we hear this creature approaching us. We could hear it's wings flapping rapidly. If you've ever had a hummingbird fly close to you, that's exactly what it sounded like.

It seemed to try to land on Brandon's head, so he raised his arm up above his head and swatted his arm downward. As in, such a downward motion, that it would've projected this creature right into the path of my leg that was crossed over my other leg.

In this exact moment, due to the extreme swatting motion going on, Brandon spilled his coffee, which ran down my shin and pooled into my house shoe.

Not being able to see, and feeling this warm substance run down my leg, combined with the projectile swatting path, I was convinced this unknown creature had landed on my shin and was drawing blood, which was why I felt such warmness running down my leg.

So, I did what any normal person would do in this situation...

I sat frozen, yelling "It's on me!", over and over again.

My now-soaked pajama pants had gripped onto my leg, which was why I was convinced "it" was still attached to me.

Unbeknownst to me, Brandon knew exactly what had happened, and at the same time I'm yelling "it's on me!", he is yelling, "it's coffee!".

Repeat this scenario a couple times.

It was not until Brandon touched my arm and got my full attention, that I was able to hear him, and understand that it was not a blood-sucking fire-breathing hummingbird attacking me, but rather just plain-ole warm coffee.

Once realization registered on my face, we both dissolved in laughter.

Here's the thing though, it was amazing

that I was so caught up in my coffee-soaked pajama-pant crisis, that I couldn't even hear Brandon telling me what was really happening. In that moment, I couldn't hear his voice, which was the voice of truth in the situation. When the coffee attacked, I was way too caught up in the moment to position myself to listen.

Man, oh man, I have done this EXACT same thing in life. I've been so caught up in a stressful season, a rage-filled moment, a crisis where "life" attacked, and I didn't know what to do, that I couldn't even hear The Voice of Truth, my Lord Jesus Christ.

This was such a tangible lesson to learn if I would JUST STOP. Just be still. Just pause. And position myself to hear The Voice of Truth, how differently would I be able to see my situation?

Very different.

When you and I take the time-out to seek wisdom, we are promised that we will find it.

And, that's good news for the next time a blood-sucking, fire-breathing hummingbird, coffee, or LIFE attacks!

"Then you will call upon Me and come and pray to Me, and I will listen to you. You will seek Me and find *Me* when you search for Me

with all your heart. I will be found by you,'
declares the Lord, 'and I will restore your
fortunes and will gather you from all the
nations and from all the places where I have
driven you,' declares the Lord, 'and I will
bring you back to the place from where I sent
you into exile.'"
Jeremiah 29:12-14

CPSIA information can be obtained
at www.ICGtesting.com
Printed in the USA
FSOW04n1133121116
27250FS